her cold martini

haiku

Marsh Muirhead

Great to see you again!

Marsh Muirhead
KW '24

her cold martini
haiku

© 2013 Marsh Muirhead
The Island Journal Press
5745 River Park Rd NE
Bemidji, Minnesota 56601
mgmuirhead@midco.net

ISBN 978-0-9814995-4-3

Printed in the United States of America
Arrow Printing, Inc.
PO Box 609
Bemidji, Minnesota 56601
Cover Design by Emily Nordstrom

Acknowledgements:

Acknowledgement is made to the editors of the following journals in which most of the haiku in this collection first appeared, sometimes in other versions: *Acorn, bottle rockets, Frogpond, The Heron's Nest* and *Modern Haiku*. Others were first published or reprinted in the Sunday edition of *The Key West Citizen*.

Modern Haiku awarded "her cold martini" the favorite Senryu for the summer 2008 issue. It also appeared in *White Lies - The Red Moon Anthology of English-Language Haiku*, 2008, Jim Kacian-editor. The poem was later aired and published on the video poetry website *Howpedestrian.ca* (Toronto, Canada) in July of 2010.

Frogpond published "after she leaves" in the autumn 2012 issue, and for that appearance received the Museum of Haiku Literature Award, made possible by the Museum of Haiku Literature, Tokyo, Japan.

The Robert Frost Poetry Festival awarded "longest night of the year" (2008), and "last night of the carnival/traces of sweetness" (2013), finalist prizes for their annual contest. The poems are published on the website and in the newsletter and anthologies for those events.

Other haiku have appeared in the following anthologies: *Carving Darkness - The Red Moon Anthology of English-Language Haiku*, 2011, Jim Kacian-editor; *Haiku 21 - An Anthology of Contemporary English-Language Haiku*, 2011, Lee Gurga and Scott Metz-editors; *Nothing in the Window - The Red Moon Anthology of English-Language Haiku*, 2012, Jim Kacian-editor; and in *The Temple Bell Stops - Contemporary Poems of Grief, Loss, and Change*, 2012, Robert Epstein-editor.

her cold martini
the olive
looks at me

night-blooming basswoods
how easy it should be
to fall in love

                              Independence Day
                              my oldest
                              asks for a loan

autumn equinox
salamanders cross the road
from both sides

October moon
everything
on this side or the other

skinny dipping
in a mountain creek
just me and this ouzel

foghorn
floating somewhere
thirty tons of ore

anniversary dance
just us
across the tongue and groove

baggage claim
overdressed
for her luggage

waiting for the drawbridge
the subject
we won't discuss

longest night of the year
no answer
for the owl

unanswered loon
moon
across the water

summer squall
lily pads
hold the pond in place

all-night drive
braking for the deer
that isn't there

the lake cracks
at twenty below
sound of water

autumn rain
taps the fallen leaves
property taxes due

roadside sweet corn
the girl tans her legs
next to the money

a school bus
grinds its gears
the bully inside

last week of school
history
slows to a crawl

her last breath winter rain

between fence rails
the little boy
explains cows to the cows

wearing his life jacket
the little boy
runs through the sprinkler

new girl
at the grocery
I stand in the longest line

trying to mingle
with spring breakers
the waitress calls me sir

big wedding dance
x's
dance with x's

nephew's girlfriend
my best lines
on the tip of my tongue

coffee shop date jitters

May-December romance
she talks her way
into the money

skinny dipping
in the hot tub
more than a full moon

spring picnic
under the slippery elm
he makes his move

late night groceries
checking out
the ring fingers

scent of her wet swimsuit when it's off

agreeing
to Christian singles night
I change my sheets

I can't see you now she says meaning ever

three a.m.
the call that doesn't come
fills the house

Atlanta flight delay
low visibility
in the smoking lounge

                              floating the afternoon
                              on this raft
                              still unemployed

second day in Key West
eating pink shrimp
the pink tourist

bridges to Key West
the water
too many blues to name

hopping around
in Sloppy Joe's
the other leg in Iraq

throbbing headache
unable to see
what was so funny

martini Monday
the dog
sleeps in another room

night sweats
the chemistry
of regret

dry mouth
full bladder
wrong house

again I won't do this again

taste
of the memory
of the wine

pruning the apple tree
I let go
my argument

flight to Cancun
my tongue in the hole
in the ice cube

the facts of life
slide under the child's door
cocktail party

chopping wood his splintering rage

scything
thistles
if
only   easy
it   that
were

point zero two
interest
daylight savings

the gentler bite of a pit bull's love

Christmas tree
wrong from every angle
trial separation

invited to
share the peace
I loosen my tie

someone's last first cicada

wild iris
on the river bank
shall I stay or go?

produce aisle
not buying an eggplant
all my life

father's funeral
closed casket
open bar

after she leaves
the weight
of hanging apples

last night of the carnival
the rising cost
of the Teddy bear

last night of the carnival
traces of sweetness
tug at my flip flops

last night of the carnival
the tilt-a-whirl
whirling empty

Author's Note:

In January of 2007, at the Key West Literary Seminar, Billy Collins assigned our poetry workshop the task of beginning each day with a 17-syllable haiku - an exercise to prime the pump of image and concision. Three months later, in a quite serendipitous sequel to that workshop, in the gardens of The Oldest House in Key West, Charlie Trumbull, editor of *Modern Haiku*, delivered a day-long workshop on the history and practice of these easy to write (but almost impossible to write well) dense three-liners. I have since found writing haiku a maddening, but rewarding exercise in opening those tiny windows into the truth about the way we connect with our natural world and the people around us.

I would like to thank Charlie for his advice on selections for this book, and for his continued support, mentoring and friendship since that first meeting. In a few cases, I went against Charlie's advice and included haiku that he did not strongly support. Any weaknesses in this collection are of my own doing.

In 2010 Billy Collins came to Bemidji for "An Evening with the Former U.S. Poet Laureate," which also featured a craft lecture and social events. At his reading (which drew the usual standing ovation), Billy read his very moving and entertaining poetry, as well as haiku from his book *She Was Just Seventeen* (Modern Haiku Press, Lincoln, Illinois). It was a memorable weekend for our community, and I thank Billy for sharing with us his work, insights, and humor.

A note of appreciation to Midwest Regional Coordinator for the Haiku Society of America, Charlotte Digregorio, who contributed her time in helping select particular haiku, for her advice on the publishing and construction of this book, and for her discussion and support of my work on her Writer's Blog.

Finally, I extend a warm thank you to the extended members of my growing haijin (a writer of haiku) family who, either in person or from afar, acted as a teacher, critic, editor or supporter, often in ways in which they were not aware.

About the Author:

Marsh Muirhead is a writer, pilot and flight instructor, dentist and former bodybuilder (Mr. Minnesota, 1983, light heavyweight class) - although the evidence for this is diminishing. He won the 2011 Great American Think-Off, answering the question, "Does Poetry Matter?" He said it does. He is the Benevolent Dictator of The Island Republic, an island nation of three acres, the first island in the Mississippi River, near Bemidji, Minnesota. His poems and stories have appeared in *Rattle, The Southeast Review, Carolina Quarterly, New Mexico Poetry Review, North Dakota Quarterly, The Talking Stick,* and other journals. He is the author of *Key West Explained - a guide for the traveler,* available at Amazon Books. He can be reached at mgmuirhead@midco.net.